Wales Coast Path: Pembrokeshire Coastal
Viewpoints

Text: Dennis Kelsall
Series editor: Tony Bowerman
Photographs: © Crown copyright (2020) Visit Wales, Dennis Kelsall, Shutterstock, Dreamstime, Alamy, Adobe Stock, Drew Buckley

Design: Carl Rogers and Laura Hodgkinson

© Northern Eye Books Limited 2020

Northern Eye Books

ISBN 978-1-908632-93-7

A CIP catalogue record for this book is available from the British Library.

www.walescoastpath.co.uk

Cover: Carn Llidi (Walk 5)

Important Advice: The routes described in this book are undertaken at the reader's own risk. Walkers should take into account their level of fitness, wear suitable footwear and clothing, and carry food and water. It is also advisable to take the relevant OS map with you in case you get lost and leave the area covered by our maps.

Whilst every care has been taken to ensure the accuracy of the route directions, the publishers cannot accept responsibility for errors or omissions, or for changes in the details given. Nor can the publisher and copyright owners accept responsibility for any consequences arising from the use of this book.

If you find any inaccuracies in either the text or maps, please write or email us at the address below. Thank you.

First published in 2020 by

Northern Eye Books Limited
Northern Eye Books, Tattenhall, Cheshire CH3 9PX

tony@northerneyebooks.com
For sales enquiries, please call 01928 723 744

www.northerneyebooks.co.uk

Printed and bound in the UK by Severn, Gloucester

Instagram: @wales_coast_path
@northerneyebooks

Twitter: @WalesCoastUK
@northerneyeboo

Contents

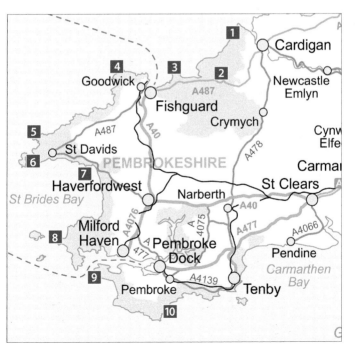

The Pembrokeshire Coast

DEFINING THE SOUTH-WESTERNMOST TIP OF WALES, Pembrokeshire's coastline is arguably the most beautiful and varied in the British Isles. Virtually all of it lies within the Pembrokeshire National Park. Relative isolation has left it largely untouched by modern development and most of its length is a wild frontier where the endless confrontation between sea and land is played out. Long stretches of coast face the fury of Atlantic storms and weakness and faults in the high cliffs are eroded into caves, coves and inlets. However, the harder rock, some of which is 700 million years old, resists the onslaught and stands out in rugged promontories and headlands. Elsewhere, sheltered landings and harbours, fine beaches and secluded bays reveal other aspects of this glorious landscape. In spring and summer the cliff tops break out in the pink, blue, white and yellow of countless flowers and sea crags are alive with nesting birds, while some of Britain's largest seal populations arrive in autumn to give birth.

Skomer Island emerges from the mist across Jack Sound

Pembrokeshire's coastal views

For some hillwalkers, the 'view' is only achieved on attaining the summit. But here, the endless convolutions of the coastline create an ever changing scene, both in front and behind; with every step shifting the perspective, bringing something different into sight. While the distant view can stretch for miles, inlets, coves and bays may remain hidden, only revealing themselves at the last moment. More immediately, the cliffs are broken by crevices, ledges, caves and natural arches, while just offshore are stacks and wave-washed shoals.

Behind, the hinterland is a patchwork of hill, common and agriculture, while the vista out to the sea is endlessly changed by the weather, tide and hour. And, where accessible, the prospect from the beach is different again.

"The sea, once it casts its spell, holds one in its net of wonder forever."

Jacques Cousteau

TOP 10 Walks: Coastal views

WHILE BEAUTY IS SAID TO LIE IN THE EYE OF THE BEHOLDER, there can be no doubt that these walks lead through some of the Pembrokeshire's finest scenery. Views range from craggy headlands to sheltered beaches, and wooded valleys to open heath. And there are forays onto coastal hills too.

None of the walks are overly long, yet at any time of the year, there is much to see and they are not to be hurried.

Cemaes Head — page 8

Carn Ingli — page 14

Dinas Head — page 20

Strumble & Garn Fawr — page 24

St David's Head & Carn Llidi page 30

Ramsey Sound page 36

St Brides Bay page 42

Marloes Peninsula page 46

Angle Peninsula page 52

Stackpole Head page 58

Cemaes Head is characterised by heavily twisted and buckled sedimentary rocks

Cemaes Head

A superb walk featuring the highest point along the Pembrokeshire Coast Path

What to expect:
Generally good field paths, tracks and coast path, a couple of sustained ascents

Distance/Time: 7 kilometres/ 4½ miles. Allow 2 to 2½ hours

Start: Allt-y-coed Farm (donations for parking)

Grid ref: SN 134 493

Ordnance Survey map: Explorer OL35 (North Pembrokeshire)

Refreshments: The Webley Hotel, Poppit Sands SA43 3LN | 01239 612085 | www.webleyhotel.co.uk OR The Ferry Inn, St Dogmaels SA43 3LF | 01239 615172 | www.ferryinn.wales

Walk outline

Leaving Allt-y-coed, the route sets off south across fields and along forgotten lanes to Cwm yr Esgyr, through which it drops to Gernos. Rising beyond the farm, the walk reaches Graig, where it turns and falls above a side stream to join the Coast Path behind Pwllygranant. The way then climbs above Pembrokeshire's highest cliffs to Cemaes Head, there turning the point for the final leg, which overlooks the Teifi estuary.

The views

The highest point of the whole Pembrokeshire Coast Path lies between Pwllygranant and Cemaes Head, and gives a superb view back along the coast past Dinas Island to Strumble Head. Just around the point, the prospect is across Cardigan Bay to the mountains of Snowdonia, some 70 miles distant. But it is the closer sights that make this walk truly spectacular. The sedimentary rocks of the Cemaes headland are buckled and folded in a most dramatic manner and, exposed to the full force of Atlantic gales, the relatively soft rock has been pounded and undercut to create high, precipitous cliffs behind Traeth y Rhedyn and Traeth Godir-côch.

High cliffs

Fulmar

uphill beside a couple of fields. Climbing out over a stile in the corner onto a track, turn right. A short distance along, look for a stepped stile on the left. Head out towards a **belt of pine**, passing through to walk on at the edge of another field.

2. Joining a track from **Pengarn-fâch**, follow it over a **cattle grid**. At the far end of a long field by a **three-way signpost**, pass through a gate on the right from which a track curves down the hill. Beyond another gate continue the descent to a junction by the derelict **Bryn Salem chapel**. *The chapel was built in 1852 and subsequently renovated during the 1920s when a new organ was installed. During the 1950s, despite a scattered community and another chapel at nearby Cippyn, it had a congregation of 45, but 30 years later there were so few that the church had become unviable and it has been empty since 1983.*

The Walk

1. Walk up the access track back to the **hairpin**. Just to the right, a path is signed left up steps within a small plantation. Emerging at the top, go right through a gate and immediately left to continue

3. Go right along an old, hedged track. Approaching a gate barring the way, cross a stile on the left. Head downfield

0   1 km

                 ½ mile

The Wales Coast Path zig-zags down a steep slope into Pwllygranant

then curve right beside a **conifer plantation**. The path slants into the trees, emerging at the bottom onto a farm track. Follow it right along the valley.

4. After 200 metres, shortly before the **farm at Gernos**, leave over a stile on the left. Walk down across the base of the valley, rising beyond to swing right beside another plantation above the farm. Where the way later levels to a junction, keep ahead to a stile. Carry on at the edge of a couple of fields to come out onto a track at **Graig**. Cross another stile diagonally opposite to reach a second track.

5. Turn left, but then abandon it after a few metres over a stile on the right. Follow the hedge down, bearing right beyond its end to the bottom corner. A path winds on, initially within a wooded fold then across bracken to a **footbridge**. Continue down to meet the **Coast Path**.

In June 1993, a heatwave ended in torrential thunderstorms along much of the Welsh coast. Six inches of rain fell in just a few hours, causing many disastrous floods including here, where the otherwise innocuous stream stripped bare much of the valley's lush vegetation.

An acute fold in the Silurian sedimentary rocks below Cemaes Head

6. Climb steeply to the right, the increasing height opening the view south along the coast. Leaving the valley, attention ahead is then grabbed by the cliffs above Traeth y Rhedyn. Beyond a dip, another corner brings the run of cliffs behind Traeth Godir-côch into view.

If such a statistic has any meaning, the average elevation of the Pembrokeshire Coast Path is around 115 feet (35 metres), with cliffs typically standing around 150 feet (45 metres) above the sea. But the many ups and downs mean that completing the 186 mile trail involves a total climb (and descent) of around 35,000 feet (10,687 metres), considerably more

than the height of Everest. The stretch here includes the highest point along the whole Pembrokeshire coast and comes on either the first or last day of the walk. With steep climbs culminating at just over 570 feet (175 metres) it presents one of the challenges of the walk and is a factor for many in deciding which direction to tackle the route.

Keep going through a gate, shortly reaching a stile. The way lies to the left, dropping across a broad shelf and then on past an old lookout, where the falling hillside opens a panorama across Cardigan Bay. Eventually through a field gate, go left to a small gate onto the **Cemaes Head National Nature Reserve**.

7. The open ground slopes down to sheer cliffs buttressing the point, but the way lies right to another gate. Swing right again on a path overlooking the Teifi estuary to Cardigan Island. Leaving the reserve, follow the ongoing track towards **Allt-y-coed**. Through a gate at the end, go left and right to pass through the **farmyard** and back to the parking area to complete the walk. ♦

Cemaes Head

Steep grassland and heath falling to sheer cliffs on either side of the headland, the Cemaes Head National Nature Reserve is abundant in bird and plant life. Along the cliffs, choughs, fulmars, shags and cormorants all breed while the more sheltered areas harbour wheatears, skylarks and stonechats. Look seaward and you might spot dolphins or porpoise and, as summer fades, more seals come here to breed than anywhere else along the Welsh coast.

Looking down on Newport from the rocky summit of Carn Ingli

Carn Ingli

From a spectacular outlier of the Preseli Hills to the cliffs of Newport Bay

What to expect:
Undulating paths after a steady climb to the top of Carn Ingli.
NOT advised in poor visibility

Distance/Time: 12.5 kilometres/ 7¾ miles. Allow 3½ to 4 hours

Start: Parrog car park (pay and display)

Grid ref: SN 051 396

Ordnance Survey map: Explorer OL35 (North Pembrokeshire)

Refreshment: Morawelon Waterfront Bar and Restaurant, Parrog | 01239 820565 | www.campsite-pembrokeshire.co.uk OR The Golden Lion, Newport | 01239 820321 | www.thegoldenlion.co.uk

Walk outline

After following the estuary to Pen-y-Bont, the path turns inland past a prehistoric dolmen around the edge of town. A sustained pull up the open hillside leads onto Carn Ingli, but then easy moorland paths connect the neighbouring outcrops. Dropping from the hill, tracks and paths wind past old enclosures to Holm House and the main road. The onward route winds through Cwm Rhigian to the coast for a splendid cliff-top finale back to Parrog.

The views

Carn Ingli, sometimes translated as 'Angel Mountain', is the gnarled root of an ancient volcano, one of several strung out to the west. It attracted prehistoric communities, and traces of enclosures, burials and huts scatter the hillside. It is also where the 5th-century St Brynach came to seek solitude and spiritual renewal and, being the highest point in Pembrokeshire away from the main Preseli ridge, affords an unrivalled panorama from St David's Head to Snowdonia. The coast reveals views of a different kind, with a succession of inaccessible bays and a splendid view across the Nevern estuary to Newport Sands.

Carreg Coetan

Carn Ingli wild pony

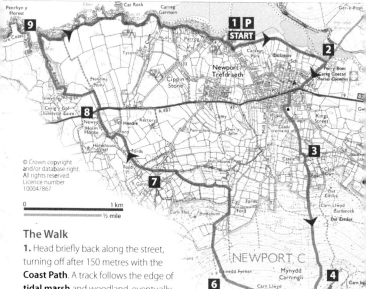

The Walk

1. Head briefly back along the street, turning off after 150 metres with the **Coast Path**. A track follows the edge of **tidal marsh** and woodland, eventually ending at a lane beside **Pen-y-Bont**.

Low tide reveals a ragged row of stepping stones, the only way across before the present bridge was built in 1894. An earlier medieval structure was demolished in the 17th century, reputedly in an attempt to keep plague from the village.

Walk away from the **bridge**, passing a street off right, which leads to **Carreg Coetan**, *an impressive Neolithic burial chamber. Built around 3,500BC, the chambered tomb was originally enclosed within a cairn. It would likely have been* used over many generations as a repository for cremated remains.

2. Reaching the main road, go right past **The Golden Lion** before leaving left into **Upper St Mary's Street**. Bend right in front of the **church** and go left to continue uphill. On reaching **College Square**, branch right up a narrow lane.

**The tumbled ramparts of a large Iron Age hillfort dominate the summit of Carn Ingli**

At the top, swing left in front of a house and then turn off right onto a rising track, which leads to the open common.

3. Climb the clear path ahead towards **Carn Ingli**, _occasionally pausing to appreciate the retrospective view across the Nevern estuary_. Ignore crossing paths as you gain height, eventually reaching a **clump of rocks** where the path divides. Stay with the left branch, which steepens before easing as it draws level with the top of the hill that lies over to the left. Walk on to a crossing path and go left, meandering through the fringing rocks to explore the **top of Carn Ingli.**

4. Return to the crossing and now keep ahead towards a **prominent cairn**. Take the right branch at a clear fork, winding past the rocks and on to a **second cairn** _that marks an Iron Age burial on the rounded summit of the hill_.

5. Now gently falling, the ongoing path continues past **Carn Llŵyd** towards a further group of rocks, **Carnedd Fychan**. As you approach, watch for a path leaving to the right.

6. Aiming for the prominent outcrop of **Carn Ffoi**, it heads down the hill, joining the line of an old **boundary ditch** that

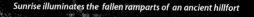

Sunrise illuminates the fallen ramparts of an ancient hillfort

leads to a gap in the wall below. Through that, bear right as the path divides and continue across a **smaller enclosure**. Exiting its far-right corner, pick up a path from the left, which in turn merges with a track dropping from the right. Continue down to pass in front of a **cottage**, there swinging left along a broad track. After 650 metres, reaching a crossing track, keep ahead and then bear left with a **bridleway** that ends past **cottages** onto a lane.

7. Cross to a track opposite. Where it forks, take the left branch to a stile and continue through **woodland**. Over another stile, carry on at the fringe of meadow and then along a watery path. Through gates at the end, go left to cross the foot of a meadow and through another **belt of trees**. Emerging beyond, turn right along the edge of grazing to leave through a gate. Follow the ongoing track out past **Holm House farm**. Approaching its end, bear off right through a hedge gap to the **main road**.

8. Cross to the track opposite, shortly going left at a junction. Reaching the entrance to **Rhigian**, take a path off right, which winds down through **woodland** to the coast.

9. Joining the **Coast Path**, climb a flight of steps onto the headland. Increasing

height gives a fine view of the inlet below, while turning the point reveals a **succession of rocky bays** to the east. After passing **Cat Rock**, the path loses height and swings above the estuary. Beyond the **old lifeboat station**, carry on along a **promenade**, which eventually drops to the **beach**. At high tide, take the waymarked 'Alternative Coast Path' route, signed off on the right. Either way takes you past **Morawelon** back to the **car park** to complete the walk. ♦

Newport

'New' was in 1197, when the town was founded by the Norman noble William Fitzmartin, as capital of the Marcher Lordship of Cemais from which he controlled the native Welsh within his domain. Overseen by a castle, originally located on the estuary downstream of Pen-y-Bont and subsequently re-established in stone on the hillside by the church, the town prospered throughout the medieval period from shipbuilding and the export of pottery and wool.

Looking north along the coast from the trig column atop Pen y Fan, on Dinas Head

Dinas Head

A short but mildly strenuous circuit to one of North Pembrokeshire's iconic viewpoints

What to expect:
A steady climb on good but occasionally exposed paths

Distance/Time: 5.25 kilometres/ 3¼ miles. Allow 1½ to 2 hours

Start: Pwllgwaelod car park

Grid ref: SN 005 398

Ordnance Survey map: Explorer OL35 (North Pembrokeshire)

Refreshment: The Old Sailors, Pwllgwaelod SA42 0SE | 01348 811491 | www.theoldsailors.co.uk

Walk outline

From the beach-head at Pwllgwaelod, the route joins the Coast Path above the western cliffs of Dinas Island to Pen y Fan, the high point on the northern tip of the headland. The return descends around the eastern flank, the lower path giving a grandstand view of Needle Rock. Dropping into Cwm-yr-Eglwys, it winds behind the ruined church before cutting back across the neck of the promontory.

The views

Flanked by Fishguard and Newport bays, Dinas Head offers unrivalled views along this section of coast. To the west, beyond Goodwick Harbour is the broad stub of the Strumble peninsula, although the lighthouse hides just behind its far point. In the other direction, Cemaes Head marks the northern-most point along the Pembrokeshire Coast Path. Inland, Mynydd Carningli (Walk 2) dominates, while behind is the higher range of Mynydd Preseli. More immediately, the high cliffs fall to inaccessible bays and coves, while barely detached from the eastern precipice is Needle Rock, a haunt for seabirds which jostle for nesting space on its narrow ledges.

Vertical strata off Dinas Head

Guillemots

The Walk

1. From the **car park**, turn right and follow a track towards **Dinas Head Farm**. Leave at a sharp right-hand bend to follow the **Coast Path** through a gate on the left. Climb on past a couple of viewpoints overlooking the coves. After the initial steep pull, the gradient eases as the path sweeps behind **Aber Penclawdd** on its way to the **trig column** marking the top of **Pen y Fan**. *Its strategic position was exploited during the Second*

World War with the construction of a lookout post, whose foundations can still be seen amongst the heather.

2. The onward path falls away in gentle descent, revealing **Needle Rock** tucked beneath the far cliffs. Closer to, approaching a gate, there is a glimpse of a smaller stack in **Pwll Glas**. The path then divides, the lower one passing directly above Needle Rock. (The right-hand branch is less rugged, taking a higher line by the fence and might be preferable in high wind.) *At another gate directly above Needle Rock, there is a fine*

Enjoying the views out to sea from Dinas Head

vantage from which to watch the comings and goings of guillemots at nesting time. Beyond, the way descends steps and soon becomes less demanding as it continues past colourful gorse, where the alternative path joins from the right. Carry on through trees before meeting a narrow lane. To the left, it leads down past **cottages** to the pretty bay of **Cwm-yr-Eglwys**.

3. Where the track swings left at the corner of the **graveyard**, a path ahead leads behind a **boat yard** to a **car park**. Carry on through a small **caravan field** to pick up the path beyond. It continues along a delightful **wooded valley**, ultimately ending at Pwllgwaelod behind **The Old Sailors**. Go left and left again back to the **car park** to complete the walk. ♦

Cwm-yr-Eglwys

Only the belfry wall of St Brynach's 12th-century chapel remains after it was destroyed in the Great Storm of October 1859, in which force 12 winds battered much of Britain's west coast, sinking around 130 vessels and claiming upwards of 800 lives. Although the sea wall was subsequently strengthened another storm 120 years later took away a section of the graveyard too. Excavations undertaken during the repairs exposed two early Christian cist burials.

Strumble Head Lighthouse stands on Ynys Meicel

Strumble & Garn Fawr

Magnificent coastal scenery with the chance of spotting seals

Distance/Time: 9.5 kilometres/ 6 miles. Allow 3 to 3½ hours

Start: Garn Fawr car park

Grid ref: SM 898 388

Ordnance Survey map: Explorer OL35 (North Pembrokeshire)

Refreshment: Café at nearby Melin Tregwynt SA62 5UX | 01348 891 288 | www.melintregwynt.co.uk

What to expect:

Generally undulating on clear paths, but with some steeper climbs

Walk outline

The walk begins over Garn Fechan then meanders through old enclosures surrounding North Pole to reach a lane near Tai-bach. The onward way descends fields towards the coast, briefly joining a track at Tresinwen before meeting the Coast Path above Porthsychan. There follows a stunning cliff-top walk, turning the point opposite Strumble lighthouse and winding on to Pwll Deri. The final stretch involves an energetic climb over Garn Fawr.

The views

Garn Fechan is one of the easiest climbs that you will ever come across, yet despite its modest height, offers one of North Pembrokeshire's most expansive panoramas. But that is no excuse for not continuing with the rest of the walk. Strumble Head's coastal cliffs are particularly impressive and the lighthouse and attendant archipelago are a gem. Further around the coast, Porth Maenmelyn and Pwll Deri with their islets are equally captivating and anywhere there is a chance of spotting a seal. Garn Fawr, the final hill, might demand a little extra effort, but the view from the top gives a glorious ending to the day.

Strumble Head walker

Male grey seal

The Walk

1. Cross the lane to a stile opposite, from which a contained path rises onto **Garn Fechan**. *The summit view towards Strumble Head is impressive, a foretaste of that to come.* The ongoing path falls to a waymarked fork. Keeping left and then left again, continue down the common to exit over a stile onto a broad track. Go right for 400 metres to find a path leaving through the left hedge bank.

2. Head away across abandoned enclosures, the path eventually winding out through a

gate onto a green swathe by **North Pole cottage**. Go left down to the lane and turn left to walk past **Tai-bach**.

3. After 200 metres, leave through a gate on the right and head down the field edge past the house. At the bottom corner, cross through a wall gap and follow a track left. Keep going from field to field and then along an old watery path, which eventually emerges onto a

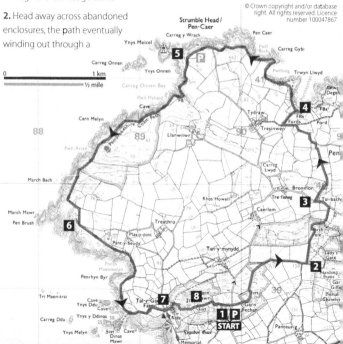

A traditional Welsh stone cottage below Garn Fawr

farm track. Walk left and then at the next junction, right. A wooded path leads down to meet the **Coast Path** above Porthsychan, where there is access to the beach.

4. The onward route, however, is left through a kissing gate onto the headland. *There is a fine view back across Fishguard Bay to Dinas and Cemaes Head with Cardigan Island in the distance, while the succession of coves below are a regular haunt for seals.* Before long, **Strumble's lighthouse** appears in front and the path passes above a **wartime lookout**,

which has been refurbished as a wildlife observatory. Joining a lane, follow it down to a small **car park**.

5. Automatically operated, there is no public access to the lighthouse across the narrow bridge that connects it to the mainland. Therefore, swing left through the car park to pick up the ongoing **Coast Path**. Progressing around **Carreg Onnen Bay**, pause for the ever-changing view back to the archipelago of small islands. Further on, behind **Pwll Arian**, springs feed a shallow, reed-filled hollow from which the path climbs around

A winter sunset colours the clifftop below Strumble Head Lighthouse

a point bringing the long line of cliffs beyond Pwll Deri into view. *Carn Llidi and St David's Head can be seen in the distance.*

6. The onward path winds behind **Porth Maenmelyn**. *The flat-roofed buildings on the hillside above were a wartime Chain Home Low radar station. It was operational between 1940 and 1946 and designed to detect the approach of low flying enemy aircraft from the sea. Beyond the cove, the stubby promontory of Dinas Mawr appears. It was the site of an Iron Age fort and the embanked rampart across the narrow neck of the isthmus can be clearly seen.* As the way then begins to rise, there is a waymarked path off right onto the promontory. Otherwise keep climbing to emerge by the white building of the **Pwll Deri Youth Hostel**. Walk out to the lane.

7. Cross to the drive opposite and wind up past **Pwll Deri Holiday Cottages**. Just before a **stone shed**, swing left on a track towards barns, but then immediately leave through a gate on the right, from which a path is signed onto the hill. At a waymarked fork higher up, keep ahead to the top of **Garn Fawr**. *This too is the site of an Iron Age settlement, its defensive stone embankments clearly visible amongst the bracken.*

8. A path off left leads to another

wartime lookout by the trig column, *where inscriptions record the builders and commanders. Beside it, a compass rose is inscribed into the rock. The views are a spectacular culmination of the walk.*

Return to the main path and continue over the top. The path winds down in a more gentle descent. Keep ahead at a later junction to return to the **car park** to complete the walk. ♦

Iron Age forts

Choosing a narrow promontory on which to create a defensible area drastically reduces the work required in creating ramparts and ditches, and over fifty such enclosures are known along the Pembrokeshire coast. The hilltop 'forts' of Garn Fawr and Garn Fechan, however, are unique on this coast and their relation to Dinas Mawr presents a mystery. Perhaps they served separate family groupings or alternatively fulfilled different purposes within a single important settlement.

Ramsey Island seen across the sound from the summit of Carn Llidi

St David's Head & Carn Llidi

Pembrokeshire's most westerly hill is steeped in prehistoric mystery

What to expect:
Good paths and tracks, occasionally rocky with some modest uphill sections

Distance/Time: 6.5 kilometres/ 4 miles. Allow 2 to 2½ hours

Start: Whitesands car park (pay and display)

Grid ref: SM 734 271

Ordnance Survey map: Explorer OL35 (North Pembrokeshire)

Refreshment: Whitesands Beach Café and Shop

Walk outline

Heading north from the car park, the route passes Porth Lleuog and Porthmelgan before embarking on a steady climb onto St David's Head. After swinging above the northern cliffs of the promontory, the way turns in towards Carn Llidi's eastern shoulder, from which a path winds onto the summit. Rather than head straight back, a more interesting finish returns to the common, revisiting the sheltered bays passed at the start

The views

When the sky is crystal clear, it is said that the Wicklow Mountains can be seen from the top of Carn Llidi. Indeed, one legend relates that St Patrick set sail from here on his evangelising mission to Ireland. Closer to home beyond Whitesands Bay, the St David's peninsula and Ramsey Island is laid before your feet, and keen eyes will readily spot the cathedral's tower. Further out to sea are scattered the wave-washed reefs known as the Bishops and Clerks. Looking east, the coast past the neighbouring hills of Carnedd-lleithr and Penberry runs all the way to the Strumble headland.

Carn Llidi, wild thyme

Stonechat

Ramsey Island peeps over the rocky summit of Carn Llidi

The Walk

1. Signed to 'St David's Head and Abereiddi', the **Coast Path** leaves the car park a short distance right of a telephone box. Rise across the neck of **Trwynhwrddyn** and behind **Porth Lleuog**, where there is a sheltered and often quiet beach. Beyond a gate, ignore a path off right and look to the skyline in front for a glimpse of Coetan Arthur, one of several burial chambers passed along the walk. The path drops to a **stream** behind **Porthmelgan**, where there is another secluded beach.

2. Cross and bear left on a path that gently gains height along the flank of the headland. Ignore a path climbing right and carry on, shortly reaching a **stone rampart**, *which was built as a defence for a small Iron Age settlement that occupied the tip of the headland. Just beyond the barricade, a sheltered area contains the foundations of several prehistoric round houses.*

3. After exploring the headland, return across the far end of the rampart to follow the ongoing path above the northern cliffs. As you pass behind the narrow cove of **Ogof Coetan**, bear off right to find the **Coetan Arthur dolmen** a little distance away, hidden among the rocks (SM 7253 2805). Return to continue with the **Coast Path**, shortly passing a **cairn** that marks the high point of the ridge. Carry on beyond, keeping left as another path joins. The way then falls to a junction.

4. Go right, but at the next junction, keep left. The path soon curves to parallel a wall and rises towards the eastern **saddle of Carn Llidi**. Approaching the crest,

watch for a distinct path branching off to the right. Gently rising, it winds across the northern flank of the hill. Ignore a couple of narrow paths that make for the rocky eastern end of the outcrop and carry on until you draw level with the high point. There, an easy path follows the line of a **shallow gully** up to a slight coll on the ridge.

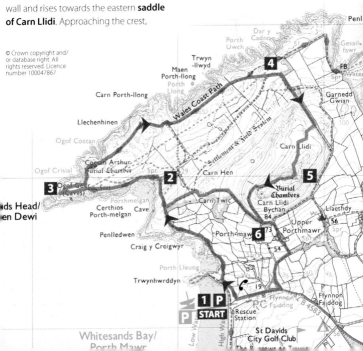

The massive capstone of Coetan Arthur, a Neolithic burial chamber on St David's Head

A glance at the map shows Carn Llidi to be just one of a sporadic line of isolated hills that stretches away to the north west. The result of ancient igneous intrusions and undersea volcanic activity, they stand proud of the surrounding landscape, where the later, softer sedimentary rocks have succumbed to erosion. The summit offers a superb vantage that takes in much of the Pembroke peninsula and, on the clearest of days, it is possible to see the Wicklow Mountains across the Irish Sea.

5. After admiring the stunning view, clamber carefully right over the rocks at the western end to find a **concrete path** that drops from the concrete foundations

of **Highwinds** below, originally a wartime submarine listening station. Follow it down to another group of foundations beside which are **two small dolmens**. The ongoing path descends through two rusting gateposts off the hill.

The volcanic outcrop underlying the peninsula continues beneath the sea, emerging as Ramsey and the scattering of small islands beyond, known as the Bishops and Clerks. Although always representing a hazard to shipping, it was not until 1839 that a lighthouse was positioned on Emsger, the South Bishop Rock.

6. Lower down, a path joins from the right. The quick way back continues

ahead, down past cottages at **Upper Porthmawr** to follow a track out to the lane above the **car park**. To linger longer on the slopes of the hill, turn sharp right over the crest of a rise. At a fork beyond the corner of a wall, keep left, soon joining another path from the right. Carry on down to an obvious junction and go left again towards the sea. Meeting the **Coast Path**, turn left and retrace your steps back to the **car park** to complete the walk. ♦

Dolmens

Arthurian references abound throughout Wales, but Coetan Arthur on St David's Head predates the legendary king by some 3,500 years. Part of a Neolithic passage grave, the massive capstone is unusually supported by only a single upright. The burial chamber, together with those on top of Carn Llidi, would originally have been covered with stones and earth and perhaps remained in use as ceremonial and burial sites into the Bronze Age.

The old harbour wall at Porth Clais was built by the Romans

Ramsey Sound

A cliff-top walk overlooking Ramsey Sound, where dolphins, seals and porpoises gather

Distance/Time: 12.5 kilometres/ 7¾ miles. Allow 3½ to 4 hours

Start: Porth Clais National Trust car park (pay and display)

Grid ref: SM 740 242

Ordnance Survey map: Explorer OL35 (North Pembrokeshire)

Refreshment: National Trust refreshment cabin at Porth Clais

Walk outline

The outward leg heads north along quiet lanes past Clegyr-Boia to Treleddyn, from which track and path lead to the coast above Porthselau's pleasant beach. The walk then follows the Coast Path around Point St John to the lifeboat station at St Justinian's and continues beside Ramsey Sound to Pen Dal-aderyn. Turning the headland, the final stretch winds behind a second beach at Porthlysgi before ultimately returning to Porth Clais.

The views

Although lacking a specific high point, an ever-changing perspective brings something new at almost every step around the coast. At first the eye is drawn back to Whitesands Bay and St David's Head, but then the craggy island nature reserve of Ramsey comes into view across the turbulent, narrow waters of its sound. Although Tenby can boast something similar, the sight of adjacent old and new lifeboat stations at St Justinian's is rather uncommon, while the bay is the departure point for boats out to the island. The tide race often attracts playful dolphins and porpoises, while spring and early summer delight with countless flowers along the cliffs.

Overlooking Ramsey Sound

Bottlenose dolphins

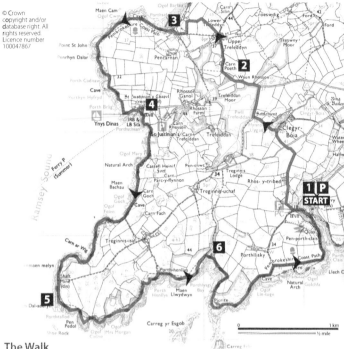

The Walk

1. Turn right out of the **car park** and follow the lane uphill. At a **crossroads**, keep ahead towards 'St Justinian's', shortly bending sharply left at **Clegyr-Boia**. Carry on to a T-junction and go left, the way again signed to 'St Justinian's'.

2. Reaching a fork, bear right, the lane becoming a track that leads to **Treleddyn**. Keep ahead between buildings, passing through a gate at the far end to continue along a field track. Approaching a **house**, turn off left at the field edge. In the next corner, go right through a gate. Cross a track to a stile opposite and walk down to a gate. Swing right to the coast.

Porthstinian's lifeboat station is the third to stand here and was opened in 2016 to

Old and new lifeboat stations at St Justinian's

house a new Tamar class boat that had arrived on station three years previously. Too big for the old boathouse, it was generally moored in the bay but its predecessor remained on standby in case Norah Wortley had to be relocated during bad weather. St David's first lifeboat, Augusta had been commissioned in 1869, a 32-foot open self-righter crewed by 10 oarsmen. Its successor in 1885 was slightly bigger, but was tragically wrecked with the loss of the coxswain and two crew members on The Bitches during a rescue attempt in 1910. An elevated boathouse and slipway were constructed for its replacement, the motor-powered General Farrell, which continued in service until 1936, saving 17 lives. Over the years four further boats successively served the area, during which time perhaps one of the most notable rescues was in 1956 when, together with the Rosslare lifeboat, 45 crew were rescued from the stricken tanker World Concord.

3. Joining the **Coast Path** above the beach at **Porthselau**, follow it left. The view to the right is across Whitesands Bay to St David's Head, while ahead are the offshore rocks of Carreg-gafeiliog.

A summer sunrise lights up Ramsey Island and St David's Head

Rounding the **point**, Ramsey Island appears across the sound. At first, the tiny bay of **Porthstinian** is hidden from sight, but a little further on, the old and new **St David's lifeboat stations** dramatically appear, perched on stilts above the cove.

4. The path winds behind the two sets of access steps to continue around the coast. Ahead, the tiny spur of **Castell Heinif** made an ideal defensible position for Celtic settlers, its narrow neck pierced by a natural arch, **Ogof Mary**. Towards the far end of the sound lies The **Bitches**, a group of rocks over which the tide can rush in a spectacular fashion.

5. Approaching the point of **Pen Dal-aderyn**, the path passes the small, fenced **shaft of an old mine**, worked for copper during the 19th century. *Opposite, the southern point of Ramsey Island fragments into a scattering of small islets, while to the south, across the broad sweep of St Brides Bay lies Wooltack Point and Skomer Island. The changing perspective then brings Porthlysgi Bay into sight and inland there is a glimpse to St David's and its cathedral.* The path drops steeply to the head of the bay. Go right to the **beach**, and then immediately left across a **stream** to walk away past a small **stone ruin**, the original St David's lifeboat station.

6. The climb back onto the cliffs is less steep and there are more fine views before the way finally turns into the long inlet of **Porth Clais.** The path ultimately drops onto the **quay** by a couple of well-preserved **lime kilns**; there are more on the opposite side of the harbour. Walk out to the lane and keep ahead back to the **car park**, to complete the walk. ♦

Ramsey Island

Once the monastic retreat of St Justinian, Ramsey was extensively farmed until 1968, when it was protected as an RSPB reserve. Amongst the many species breeding along its cliffs are peregrines, choughs, Manx shearwaters and auks, while the tiny coves and caves below serve as nurseries for the 400 or so grey seal pups born there each year. Red deer graze the hills and can sometimes be seen with binoculars from the mainland.

Solva harbour is a flooded river valley, or 'ria'

St Brides Bay

Take the Puffin Shuttle on this one-way walk from a fine beach to a picturesque harbour

What to expect:
Occasionally strenuous climbs, but clear paths throughout

Distance/Time: 7.5 kilometres/ 4¾ miles. Allow 2½ to 3 hours

Start: Duke of Edinburgh, Newgale, parking at harbour car park, Solva (pay and display)

Grid ref: Start SM 847 222 (car park SM 805 243)

Ordnance Survey map: Explorer OL35 (North Pembrokeshire)

Refreshment: Pubs and cafés at both Newgale and Solva

Walk outline

Take the Puffin Shuttle from Solva to Newgale, alighting at the 'Duke of Edinburgh Inn'. The walk briefly follows the road before climbing with the Coast Path onto the cliffs above Pwll March. The ups and downs continue around the coast, passing viewpoints at Dinas Fach, Dinas Fawr and Penrhyn. From the beachhead at Gwadn, there is a final climb over Gribin before dropping beside the long inlet of Solva's harbour.

The views

Islands bracket both jaws of St Brides Bay, Ramsey to the north and Skomer to the south. Both are bird reserves, as is Grassholm far out to sea, where the comings and goings of gannets during the breeding season are sometimes visible from the cliffs as a cloud. Within the bay itself, gas and oil tankers often anchor while awaiting their turn to dock in Milford Haven. There are impressive views along the coast too, where the mile-long stretch of Newgale's shingle bank and sandy beach contrast with the rugged cliffs that run in the opposite direction to St David's Head.

Solva dinghies

'Sea pinks' or thrift

The Walk

1. Head back across the **bridge** at the northern end of **Newgale beach** and follow the road up the hill. Watch for the **Coast Path** leaving beside a house garage on the first sharp bend. As it climbs away, pause to enjoy the expanding view back along Newgale Sands. Across St Brides Bay is the Marloes peninsula and Skomer Island with Grassholm Island on its own, far out to sea. Ahead is the St David's promontory with Ramsey Island beyond. Over the crest, the path drops steeply to the foot of **Cwm Mawr**, where there is an easy scramble onto the beach. Indeed, when the tide is safely out, you can walk on the beach from Newgale to this point.

2. The climb away with the continuing **Coast Path** is less steep, the twists, turns and undulations of the path changing the perspective of the views. Look out for the natural arch of **Ogof Felen**, the Yellow Cave; so named perhaps from the lichen growing on the rock. Beyond is the fragmented promontory of Dinas Fach, the site of an Iron Age fort whose defensive ramparts remain clearly visible.

3. The path dips behind **Porthmynawyd** before climbing past **Dinas Fach** and on to **Dinas Fawr**. *The surrounding rocks contain fractured veins of copper, lead and even silver, and intermittent small-scale mining was carried out between the 17th and 19th centuries.* There, a path balances on the narrow arête onto the spit. The view ahead now reveals Solva, although the mouth of its inlet is not yet discernible. Carry on above inaccessible

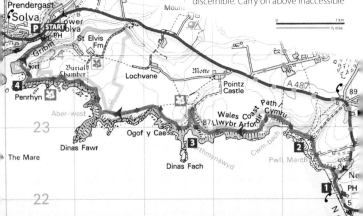

The Gribin is a rocky ridge overlooking Solva's long harbour inlet

beaches, the cliff tops ablaze with flowers during spring. The path eventually falls to a gate above **Gwadn**, but first wander left to enjoy the view from the top of Penrhyn.

4. Through the gate, drop steeply to a shingle beach in the **small cove**, crossing a stream that emanates from a long, winding valley. There is then a steep,

final pull onto **Gribin**, from where there is a splendid view of the twiasting inlet guarding Solva's natural harbour. Follow the spine away, watching for the **Coast Path** branching off left to angle down through the trees cloaking the ridge's steep flank. At the bottom, cross a **bridge** spanning the river back to the **car park** to complete the walk. ♦

Newgale beach

The striking shingle bank that runs for over a mile behind Newgale Sands is a relatively recent phenomenon, having been washed up during the Great Storm of 1859. Its existence is, however, precarious as rough seas can just as easily breach its defence to flood the land behind. Such a storm demolished the original Duke of Edinburgh inn in 1896, the present pub reputedly financed with twenty gold sovereigns salvaged from the ruins.

Mouse's Haven is a tiny cove below Wooltack Point

Marloes Peninsula

*Offshore islands and a wild, rocky Atlantic coast
with opportunities for the beach*

What to expect:
*Some steep climbs, but
good paths with short
sections along quiet
lanes*

Distance/Time: 12 kilometres/ 7¼ miles. Allow 3 to 3½ hours

Start: Runwayskiln National Trust car park (pay and display)

Grid ref: SM 779 082

Ordnance Survey map: Explorer OL36 (South Pembrokeshire)

Refreshment: The Clock House Café | 01646 635800
www.clockhousemarloes.co.uk OR Lobster Pot Inn | 01646 636233
www.thelobsterpotmarloes.co.uk

Walk outline

*Leaving the car park, the route uses lane and field paths past
Marloes Court to reach the edge of the village. There's an
optional detour to the peninsula's highpoint before dropping
to the coast above Musselwick Sands. Now on the Coast Path,
the way leads to Martin's Haven and then explores Wooltack
Point before returning above the southern cliffs to Marloes
Sands. It is then a short climb back to the car park.*

The views

Peninsulas are always a good bet for all-round views
and Marloes is no exception. The rounded highpoint of
Marloes Beacon reveals the whole promontory and looks
out to its near neighbour, Dale. The coast is no less impressive, the two sides displaying very different personalities,
with the north-facing cliffs being better sheltered from
Atlantic gales adopting a more luxuriant mantle. Not to
be missed is the circumambulation of the Deer Park, only
separated by a narrow sound from Skomer. The southern
cliffs are particularly imposing, as is the tantalisingly close
Gateholm Island. At low tide, round off the day with a walk
along Marloes Sands for a different perspective of the cliffs.

Skomer ferry, Martin's Haven

Cliff-top wildflowers

The Walk

1. Leaving the southern end of the **car park**, follow the lane for 800 metres to **Marloes Court**. Immediately beyond the farm, turn through a gate on the left and follow the field edge away to emerge over a stile onto another lane at the edge of **Marloes village**. Head left. After 300 metres, look for a waymarked gate on the right, through which the route continues. However, first you might make a short detour along the lane to the next field gate on the left. It gives access to a **trig column** marking the peninsula's highpoint, *from which there is a fine view*

north past The Nab Head to the St David's peninsula on the far side of St Brides Bay. To the west beyond Wooltack Point is Skomer Island.

2. Return to go through the gate passed earlier. A contained path heads towards the coast, bending at the far end to a fork. *To visit the beach, take the right hand branch and then turn off left a little lower down. However, exercise caution as incoming tide quickly isolates the access.* The onward route undulates along the **Coast Path** to the left. At first there are views of **Musselwick Sands**, the way continuing above grassy cliffs which are particularly colourful when the spring flowers are in bloom. Eventually, **Martin's Haven** appears, the path shortly

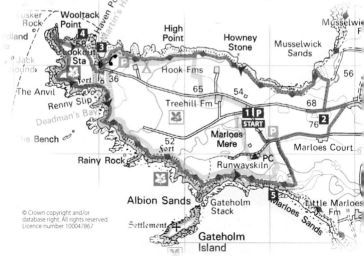

© Crown copyright and/or database right. All rights reserved. Licence number 100047867

Sunset over Skomer, The Neck, and tiny Midland Isle

dropping through a **flight of steps** to the head of the beach. *The jetty is the embarkation point for boat trips to Skomer and Skokholm islands.*

3. Leave along the climbing track, which leads past **toilets** and an **information centre** to the end of a lane. Look out for an **irregular boulder** set within a niche in the wall. *Incised with a cross, it perhaps marked a prayer station for 10th-century pilgrims landing in the cove. It was discovered in the foundation of the wall when the toilets were being constructed in 1984.* Swing around the bend at the top to visit **Lockley Lodge**, *where there is information about the Skomer and Skokholm reserves and ferry tickets can be booked.* Otherwise, pass through a gate on the right into the **Deer Park**. Fork right through an **Iron Age rampart**, the climbing path leading to a **lookout post** on top of the hill. *There you can gaze back across the whole sweep of St Brides Bay or look out to the islands.*

Some 7 miles beyond Skomer lies the tiny island of Grassholm, which has never been permanently settled and since 1947 has been in the care of the RSPB. It is home

Dramatic saw-toothed sedimentary rocks on Marloes beach

to one of the world's largest gannetries, accommodating in excess of 39,000 breeding pairs. Such is the number of birds that during the nesting season, their comings and goings appear from the mainland as a white cloud above the island

4. Carry on with the ongoing path, which drops towards **Wooltack Point**. *Overlooking the narrow sound, the cliff scenery is magnificent, with a succession of rocky coves eating into the ragged coast. As you work around the headland, look for natural arches piercing the buttresses of rock that stand from the cliffs. In time, these will collapse to leave free-standing stacks. The tiny inaccessible coves are often*

a haunt for seals. The path leaves the Deer Park through a gate. At a junction beyond, go right to continue along the coast above **Deadman's Bay**.

Further on, **behind Victoria Bay**, is the striking triple-banked defences of an **Iron Age fort**. The path runs on to a point overlooking **Gateholm Island**, which itself was the site of a Romano-British settlement that was perhaps a monastic community. *The narrow stretch of beach exposed below at low tide, Albion Sands, takes its name from the paddle steamer Albion. Passing through Jack Sound, it altered course to avoid a rowing boat and struck the Crab Stones. Although holed,*

the captain managed to beach his craft on Albion Sands, saving all hands and much of its cargo of pigs, horses and a quantity of beer and spirits. Carry on above **Marloes Sands**, the way eventually dropping to meet a path off the **beach**.

5. The way back follows the path up the hill, eventually emerging onto a lane. Go left back to the **car park** to complete the walk. ♦

Gateholm Island

Viking settlement in the area is remembered in the names of the islands Grassholm, Skokholm, Skomer and Gateholm. The latter, although barely separate from the land, is geologically distinct from the cliffs. It is formed of the same red sandstone that underlies St Ann's Head and Skokholm, rather than the older volcanic rock of the peninsula that runs from St Ishmaels to the distant offshore rocks of The Smalls.

Marram grass bows in the wind at the back of the beach at Freshwater West

Angle Peninsula

A rugged Atlantic coast is exchanged for the sheltered natural harbour of Milford Haven

Distance/Time: 15 kilometres/ 9½ miles. Allow 4½ to 5 hours

Start: West Angle car park

Grid ref: SM 854 031

Ordnance Survey map: Explorer OL36 (South Pembrokeshire)

Refreshment: The Old Point House, Angle Point | 01646 641205 www.theoldpointhouseangle.co.uk OR Wavecrest Café, West Angle Bay | 01646 641457 | www.wavecrestangle.co.uk

Walk outline

Tackling the more strenuous leg first, the route leaves West Angle Bay to climb around the coast past the East Block House. It continues along the peninsula's southern cliffs to Gravel Bay before turning inland past Rocket Cart House to Angle Bay. The way skirts the edge of the inlet to the village and then around to The Old Point House. The final stretch runs past Angle's lifeboat station and two Napoleonic forts before curving back into West Angle.

The views

Battered by Atlantic winter storms, the southern flank of the Angle peninsula is a long run of ragged cliffs and inaccessible bays with offshore rocks and small stacks that offer ideal perches for resting sea birds. The wider views extend across the fine surfing beach of Freshwater West to Linney Head, part of a military training range. By contrast, the northern coast borders Angle Bay and Milford Haven estuary, the first fringed by a broad muddy beach that attracts waders, while the Haven is one of the finest deep water anchorages in the world, a harbour for giant gas and oil tankers as well as the Irish Ferry.

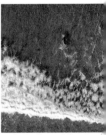

Surfer, Freshwater West

Redshank

The Walk

1. Join the **Coast Path** beside the **Wavecrest Café** and climb away at the edge of successive fields above the bay. Eventually passing into scrub, the way skirts the overgrown **Victorian East Block House** gun battery to the ruin of a **Tudor block house** on the crumbling cliffs of the point.

2. Walk on above the rocky coast, soon dropping to cross the outflow of a **stream**. *Look across as you descend to see a massive gape in the opposite slope, a collapsed cave.* The ongoing path climbs above it to continue around **Castles Bay**. At the far side a spit of rock reaches out to **Sheep Island**, the narrow gap separating it from the mainland covered at high tide. *Beyond Parsonsquarry Bay, a ruined octagonal tower of brick and stone served as a coastal*

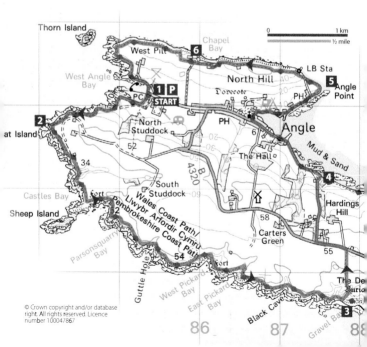

Surfer enjoying the sunset at Freshwater West

lookout, while just inland was a wartime airfield. Predominantly a fighter base used by both the Air Force and Navy, it was not finally decommissioned until the early 1950s. As you leave the next bay, look back to see Guttle Hole, an impressive fissure that completely pierces the rock. Further on, the path climbs beside **West Pickard Camp**, an Iron Age fortification whose single rampart and ditch remain clearly evident. The foundation ruins beside it were part of **RAF Angle**. Although the going remains strenuous, there is plenty of interest in the colours and striation of the rock as well as the view ahead to the popular surfing beach of Freshwater West. Eventually, after crossing a stile, the path curves in a dip behind **Gravel Bay**.

3. There, look for a path signed off through a gate on the left. It leads up a **shallow valley** to reach a crop field. Strike directly across to a gap in the far boundary and continue at the edge of a second field to emerge onto a lane near the **Rocket Cart House**. Go left and take the next right. At its end, bear right of a gated drive along a wooded track to the shore.

4. Follow the **Coast Path** left around the perimeter of **Angle Bay**, eventually

Thorn Island fort once guarded the entrance to Milford Haven

entering the **village of Angle**. Beyond the first few houses and before reaching the **church**, turn right on a track signed to 'The Old Point House'. Cross the **stream** at the head of the bay below the **castle** and then branch right above the shoreline towards **Angle Point**. Bearing right at a fork, pass in front of the **pub**. Stay by the hedge through the **car park** and continue in the fields beyond. The view over the hedge is to Fort Popton and the Valero oil refinery.

5. Just before the corner in the second field, a path leaving through a gap in the hedge leads to the ruin of Angle's first **lifeboat station**. The route, however,

remains within the field, climbing to a gate. Cross a track, walking on above the present **lifeboat station** and at the edge of successive meadows before passing into the fringe of a wind-blown, stunted sycamore wood. Beyond the trees, join a track past a couple of cottages to emerge at the end of a lane at **Chapel Bay Fort**.

During the 19th century, there was a real fear of French invasion, and Lord Palmerston, the then Prime Minister commissioned a string of coastal defences to protect the country. More than a dozen forts, blockhouses and gun batteries including installations on Thorn Island and Stack Rock and a couple of so-called martello towers in Pembroke Dock

were sited around Milford Haven to guard the ports and naval dock yards.

6. Cross to wind past the fort and on to the point where a second fort occupies **Thorn Island**. **West Angle Bay** then comes into view, the path meandering down to the **car park** at the head of the bay to complete the walk. ♦

Angle lifeboats

With a naval dockyard, trans-Atlantic and Irish ports and, more latterly, oil and gas terminals, Milford Haven has long been a busy waterway with the potential for maritime disaster. Angle's seamen were accorded honours for sea rescue well before the first lifeboat station was established on Angle Point in 1868. It was relocated 50 years later a short distance to the west, next to the present station which was opened in 1992.

Waves surge around a rock stack at Stackpole

Stackpole Head

Through lush, lakeside woodland to beautiful beaches and stunning cliffs

What to expect:
Clear paths and tracks with a short section amongst dunes

Distance/Time: 10.5 kilometres/ 6½ miles. Allow 3¼ to 4 hours

Start: Stackpole Court National Trust car park (pay and display)

Grid ref: SR 974 957

Ordnance Survey map: Explorer OL36 (South Pembrokeshire)

Refreshment: The Boathouse Tea-room, Stackpole Quay | 01646 623110 | www.nationaltrust.org.uk/stackpole

Walk outline

From the site of the former mansion, the route traces the wooded flank of the Lily Ponds' eastern valley to the coast at Broad Haven. After climbing through sand dunes onto Saddle Point, it continues above sheer cliffs around Stackpole Head to lovely Barafundle Bay. A final run of cliffs takes the way to Stackpole Quay. The return follows a track across the former deer park and then back beside the lake.

The views

The views begin at once with a lovely prospect from the old mansion's terrace along the Bosherton Lily Ponds past Eight Arch Bridge. But the real gems occur along the limestone cliffs, where erosion has created a succession of lovely bays and coves. Pounding waves have exploited weaknesses to form countless fissures, arches, stacks and caves, some of which have collapsed to produce spectacular sink holes in the headland behind. The process continues as undercut cliffs and stacks fall into a litter of tide-washed boulders far below. Barafundle Bay, backed by dunes is quite idyllic while the tiny tidal harbour and view along the coast at Stackpole Quay is a delight.

Bosherton Lily Ponds

Puffin in breeding plumage

The Walk

1. From the car park ticket machine, walk to a **four-way signpost** and go left. Breaking from the trees, cross grass to a wall at the far side, where there is a captivating view along the lake past **Eight Arch Bridge**. *The large building set back at the end of the grass is the old stable block, now converted into residential flats, but the smaller group of buildings stood adjacent to the main house and comprised*

the game larder, brew house and dairy, in which there is now a small presentation of the estate's history.

Emerging from the **exhibition**, the onward path is signed to 'Broadhaven'. Where it immediately splits, bear left, winding steeply down through trees to the lake. There, go right, shortly reaching a **boat house**, part of which has been adapted as a bird hide. Continue by the water's edge to **Eight Arch Bridge**.

Derived from Norse words meaning 'isolated rock' and 'small inlet', the Stackpole estate dates back to the 12th century, when it was settled by Elidur, a Norman knight. By the middle of the seventeenth century, it was held by the Lorts, and then by marriage to the Campbells, Lords of Cawdor, whose family seat lies in Scotland. In 1735, they built the last great house here,

Eight Arch Bridge spans the Bosherton lily pools

Stackpole Court, landscaping and planting the surrounding acres, while the valley below was flooded to create the idyllic Bosherston Lakes.

The Second World War brought everything to an end; much of the farmland, on which the estate relied for its upkeep, was requisitioned by the army, while the house itself suffered greatly as a billet for soldiers. The family never returned and the house was finally demolished in 1963 by the fifth Earl, who bequeathed the remainder of the estate to the National Trust on his death in 1970.

2. Remaining on this bank, carry on along the **lakeside**, soon reaching a causeway, **Grassy Bridge**. Cross here and follow the ongoing path beside reed beds towards the foot of the lakes. At a junction part way along, take the path off left signed to 'Stackpole Quay'. The way soon fragments, but keep ahead, rising onto an **outcrop of limestone** that gives a grandstand view back along the lakes and over Broad Haven beach.

3. Walk on over the outcrop, joining an **old estate wall** to a kissing gate. Keep ahead onto **Saddle Point**, the

Barafundle Bay is often voted one of Britain's best beaches

increasing height opening views west to the Castlemartin army range. *Offshore is the distinctive islet of Church Rock.*

A cliff-top path continues around the headland to the first of a succession of inaccessible bays, each with its own character. *Deep hollows set back from some of them are sink holes and collapsed sea caves, where the sea has exploited weakness in the rock below. In time, they too will become coves, slowly widening and eating back into the headland. Elsewhere are stacks, isolated spurs that have become completely detached from the cliff, left behind after the eventual collapse of a natural arch. The most dramatic examples*

of this in action can be seen at the tip of Stackpole Head. Around the point are more natural arches at **Griffith Lorts Hole**. Just beyond, through a gate, the path drops through a **sycamore wood** to the beach at **Barafundle**.

4. Head across the sand to leave up a **flight of steps** at the far side and carry on around the coast past several smaller sink holes. The views ahead are to the sandstone cliffs of Greenala, Trewent and, in the distance, Old Castle Head. All too soon, through a gate, the path leaves the warren and descends steps to a junction. To the right is a viewpoint overlooking **Stackpole Quay**, while going the other

way and taking the right forks leads you down to the back of the bay.

5. From the bay, head back up the track, past the **National Trust café** and across a **car park**. Leave through a gate at the far end to follow a track that rises between fields ploughed out from the old estate deer park and eventually leads to **Eight Arch Bridge**. Cross the lake and turn right, reversing your outward route to **Stackpole Court** and the **car park** to complete the walk. ◆

Stackpole National Nature Reserve

The man-made and natural landscapes create a diversity of habitats that support an abundance of plant, fungus and animal life throughout the year. Along the cliffs you might spot chough and even a puffin, while the lakes attract several duck species and occasional bittern, and are home to pike and otter. In the woods, look for bats and toadstools, and everywhere you will find flowers, including the famous lilies on the ponds.

Useful Information

Visit Pembrokeshire

Pembrokeshire's official tourism website covers everything from accommodation and special events to attractions and adventure. www.visitpembrokeshire.com

Pembrokeshire Coast National Park

The Pembrokeshire Coast National Park website also has background information and practical details to help plan your visit: **www.pembrokeshirecoast.org.uk**

Tourist Information Centres

The main TICs provide free information on accommodation, transport, what's on and walking advice.

St David's - 01437 720392 - info@orielyparc.co.uk
Fishguard - 01437 776636 - fishguard.tic@pembrokeshire.gov.uk
Fishguard Harbour - 01348 872037
Milford Haven - 01437 771818 - milford.tic@pembrokeshire.gov.uk
Pembroke - 01437 776499 - pembroke.tic@pembrokeshire.gov.uk
Tenby - 01834 845040 - tenbycentre@pembrokeshirecoast.org.uk
Tenby - 01834 842404 - tenby.tic@pembrokeshire.gov.uk
Saundersfoot - 01834 813672 - saundersfoot.tic@pembrokeshire.gov.uk

Weather

Online weather forecasts are available from the Met Office at **www.metoffice.gov.uk**

Rail Travel

National Rail Enquiries on 08457 484950 or **www.nationalrail.com.uk**

Bus Travel

A dedicated bus network serves the whole of the Coast Path

Pembrokeshire Greenways - 01437 776313 - **www.pembrokeshiregreenways.co.uk/**
Traveline Cymru - 0871 200 22 33 - **www.travelinecymru.info**

Camping

Pembrokeshire is a popular camping area, with many sites owned by or affiliated to the Camping and Caravanning Club. 024 7647 542
www.campingandcaravanningclub.co.uk